A PRISONER, wanting something to do, gleaned from the sweepings of the shop floor tiny bits of glittering wire, which he deposited in a bottle. Years passed.

On the day he was freed, there was nothing to take with him to mark the passage of those years except the bottle. And so he carried it away. Back home he rose and he ate and he slept at the exact hours the warden had decreed. Too old to work anymore, he spent his days pacing, the exact space of his long confinement; four spaces forward, four spaces back, four spaces forward, four spaces back.

For want of something to do, one day he smashed the bottle to count how many bits of glittering wire he had collected. He wept. At his feet lay broken glass and a clump of wires rusted solid in the shape of a bottle.

from *Legacies, A Chinese Mosaic*, BETTE BAO LORD

# HOPE ABANDONED

HOPE AB

# ANDONED

**EASTERN STATE PENITENTIARY**

*Photographs*
Mark Perrott

*Interviews*
Hal Kirn

Published by THE PENNSYLVANIA PRISON SOCIETY *and*
THE EASTERN STATE PENITENTIARY HISTORIC SITE

*Photographs* MARK PERROTT
*Interviews* HAL KIRN
*Prologue* BETTE BAO LORD
*Introduction* HERBERT MUSCHAMP
*Graphic design* LANDESBERG DESIGN ASSOCIATES
*Silverprints* SETH DICKERMAN
*Typography* FULL CIRCLE TYPE
*Printing* HOECHSTETTER PRINTING

*Introduction copyright 1992 New York Times Company. All rights reserved.*
*Prologue copyright 1990 Alfred A. Knopf. All rights reserved.*
*Photographs copyright 1999 Mark Perrott. All rights reserved.*
*This book, or any portions thereof, may not be reproduced or transmitted in any form or by any means, electronic or mechanical, including photocopying, recording, or by any information storage and retrieval system, without permission in writing from the publisher. Photographs may not be reproduced without permission from Mark Perrott.*

LIBRARY OF CONGRESS CATALOG CARD 99-093000
ISBN 0-9670455-0-9

FIRST PRINTING
PRINTED IN USA

*Acknowledgements*

I FIRST CAUGHT SIGHT of Eastern State Penitentiary on Saturday morning, Halloween weekend, 1992. The day was flat grey and cold, punctuated by off-and-on drizzle that later turned to snow. On that day I met the two people most important to the beginnings of this project: Milton Marks and Sally Elk. Milton listened to my request to photograph, and agreed to let the work begin without condition. A few weeks later Sally met me with the key at the Fairmount gate. At dusk she returned to release me.

Many others have contributed in their own way, including Gerald Weaber, Howard Kittell, David Brownlee, Norman Johnston, Harley Trice, Caroline Boyce, Sue Van Doeren, Tom Barbush, Margo Lovelace, Vicky Clark, Ross Howell, and Rick Landesberg. Thanks to each of you.

I'm especially grateful to Mr. Herbert Muschamp, for "In Philadelphia, a Showcase of Abandoned Hopes," *New York Times*, October, 1992. His words first called me to this wonderful modern ruin. I appreciate the opportunity The New York Times Company gave us to represent these words in this new context. Thanks, as well, to Bette Bao Lord, and Alfred A. Knopf, publisher, for permission to excerpt *Legacies, A Chinese Mosaic*, and include those words as the prologue to *Hope Abandoned*.

Hal Kirn shared his own treasure, hours upon hours of transcribed interviews with former inmates, guards, and Penitentiary neighbors. Thank you, Hal, and thanks to all who shared their recollections with you. Seth Dickerman printed each photograph with a richness that resonates with all that I witnessed. Anita Driscoll gave these images and text a wonderful form. Phil Hallen wrote warmly in support of this project. Thank you, Phil, for that gift, one of so many, and for your friendship these past twenty-seven years.

The book you hold is entirely a dream come true, thanks to the faith and extraordinary generosity of the following: The Juliet Lea Hillman Simonds Foundation, Inc., the McCune Foundation, The William Talbott Hillman Foundation, Inc., and The Heinz Endowments. Thanks to each of you who, early on, found merit in this work and committed to support it.

The Pennsylvania Prison Society and the Eastern State Penitentiary Management Committee have undertaken the formidable challenge of preserving this National Historic Landmark. Thank you for the opportunity to share in your mission in this way.

Thanks again to Sally for staying with this struggle, to Sean Kelley for his wit and unyielding enthusiasm, and to Joan for her patience and understanding.

Dave Bergholz worked quietly and tirelessly to gather financial support for this book. Thank you, David, for the kindness, wise counsel, and generosity you have shown me all of my life.

MARK PERROTT, 1999

*for Ellen and Nancy*

*Introduction*

IT WAS THE LARGEST BUILDING IN AMERICA, and reputedly the most expensive. Its bold, original design influenced architecture internationally. Tocqueville came from France to study it; Dickens declared it (along with Niagara Falls) one of the two sights he hoped to see on his 1842 American tour. Today, the Eastern State Penitentiary is something of an embarrassment, an abandoned ruin overgrown with weeds. But this gloomy landmark is still worthy of wide public attention. Few buildings shed a more penetrating light on modern democracy and its discontents.

Located just a few blocks from the Philadelphia Museum of Art, Eastern State is also a museum, a showcase of lost hopes. Empty since the last prisoners departed in 1970, the prison's stone-walled cells are haunting tableaux of a failed experiment in utopian social planning. Designed in 1821 by Philadelphia architect John Haviland, Eastern State was born from the fusion of Quaker social conscience with the Enlightenment's faith in reason. Its innovative form arose from humanitarian concern for the treatment of prisoners and from philosophical speculation about the cause and cure of crime.

Few visitors today, however, will find this place either humane or reasonable. For it was here, in the city of the Liberty Bell, that the concept of solitary confinement was put to its first major test. This was the dubious achievement of the place known around the world as "the Prison at Philadelphia."

In the mid-1980s the prison, now owned by the City of Philadelphia, was the target of several redevelopment proposals, including plans for luxury housing and an urban shopping mall. All the proposals called for substantial demolition of Haviland's architecture, however, and in 1988, in response to a petition from the task force, Mayor W. Wilson Goode turned them all down pending further study.

But the popularity of Alcatraz notwithstanding, prisons make awkward landmarks. Compared to, say, a courthouse, a prison lacks the luster of civic pride. The classical form of a courthouse extols a supreme democratic virtue: the law and its impartiality, and the consent of the governed to the rules that make their liberty possible. A prison speaks of the loss of freedom. Its message is not the law but the consequences of transgressing it: guilt, disgrace, the stigma of the outlaw state.

These qualities are not easily rendered into architecture, although Piranesi, memorably, transformed Baroque court design into "imaginary prisons" of nightmarish power. Still, for a young democratic nation, dedicated to reforming society and its institutions, the prison was an irresistible challenge. What could be more idealistic than to reform a brutal institution into an enlightened system for reforming individuals?

VIEWED FROM OUTSIDE, Eastern State resembles a Gothic fortress. Square in plan, the crenelated granite walls enclose a ten-acre site. A stone tower marks the entrance; from the corners turrets rise. The design turns the form of the medieval city inside out. No hordes clamored to enter Eastern State, though the forbidding walls were designed to deter people from acts that might land them there. The massive ramparts also gave reassurance that those confined within would remain outside the city of the law abiding.

But it is inside the walls that the prison's experimental plan unfolded. Traditionally, prisons were squalid places, where people were thrown together in common rooms, often regardless of sex, age or the severity of their offenses. They were places of disorder and social neglect. By contrast, "penitentiaries" like Eastern State were places of discipline. They were built on the theory that criminals are psychological slobs, people who failed to acquire discipline early in life. Within the penitentiary's controlled environment criminals would reform themselves through penance—hence the name. The Pennsylvania Plan, as solitary (or "separate") confinement was called, took the theory a step further. Criminals would acquire discipline more readily if they were isolated from other undisciplined souls.

Philadelphia's prison officials considered several options before choosing Haviland's plan. They deliberated over a panopticon, a circular building with an observation tower in the middle, similar to the one Benjamin Latrobe had designed for Richmond Prison in 1795. Though an observation tower arises from the center of Haviland's building, this is not the true panopticon form conceived by the British political economist Jeremy Bentham. Instead of forming a circle, Eastern State's seven cellblocks—containing 250 cells altogether—radiate from the central observation tower like spokes. (Four additional blocks and other outbuildings were added later.) This plan allowed surveillance of the open yards but, unlike a panopticon, it did not permit guards to look into the cells.

Instead of the "eye of power," to use Michel Foucault's term for the technique of constant prisoner surveillance, Eastern State relied on the power of the invisible. On arriving at the prison, prisoners were hooded before being led to their cells, to prevent them from seeing where they were going. Each cell measured 8 by 12 feet and was equipped with a flush toilet and running water. A walled yard outside the cell permitted solitary exercise. An 1831 report explained: "No prisoner is seen by another, after he enters the wall. When the years of his confinement have passed, his old associates in crime will be scattered over the earth, or in the grave... and the prisoner can go forth into a new and industrious life, where his previous deeds are unknown."

It sounds a bit like heaven, and indeed the roots of the Pennsylvania Plan lay in monastic architecture and in the solitary life of Carthusian monks. Inmates at Eastern State were provided with Bibles and were expected to work at weaving and other crafts. They received regular visits from members of the Philadelphia Prison Society, the Quaker organization that had championed the creation of Eastern State. It is as if, by emulating a monastic structure, the prison could convert a criminal calling into a religious one, sinners into saints. "The Pennsylvania System is a Divine System," hailed one contemporary advocate.

But to Dickens, who visited the prison 150 years ago, the system was infernal, precisely because of its reliance on the unseen. Prisoners were invisible to the world as well as to one another, and their punishment left no visible scars. Society did not have to witness the consequences of confining people here. Dickens thought public flogging preferable to this "slow and daily tampering with the mysteries of the brain."

But the governing concept of reform hinged on that tampering: on the prison's capacity to turn the private recesses of the mind into a matter of public interest. What stands out most vividly in Dickens's account of his visit (in his "American Notes") is the eagerness of prison officials to secure the prisoners' assent to the system that held them. One inspector asks a prisoner, "Are you resigned now? Are you a better man?" A female prisoner is asked, "Are you happy here?"

Such questioning was critical to the experiment's success. By a circular logic, only the prisoners could say if the system worked. Only they could provide the evidence that, yes, they had reformed. They had acquired discipline. They had mended their ways.

If Dickens paused to visit Independence Hall and the Liberty Bell, he did not record it. From Philadelphia he traveled south to Washington, where he spent several days attending Congressional sessions at the Capitol, "a fine building of the Corinthian order, placed upon a noble and commanding eminence."

There's a logic to Dickens's itinerary that is conceptual as well as geographic, for Latrobe's 1811 design is the complement of Haviland's: both buildings are concerned with the process of self-government. Gleaming, proud, the Capitol lifts its dome high over the landscape, the public symbol of the Republic's collective mind. From the Capitol, government power radiates outward into the city along the avenues of L'Enfant's Baroque plan. Inside the building, Latrobe's interiors (inspired, in part, by Piranesi) lay out the structure of reason within which the contentious process of self-government will unfold.

At Eastern State, the Capitol's dark twin, abusers of liberty were compelled to bring themselves back into line. The sphere of this building is the private, psychological life of we, the people. Instead of radiating outward, the building presses in. It expresses its power in physical confinement, in the constant pressure it applied to the cells and their inhabitants, to the inner lives of individuals where democratic authority resides.

Herbert Muschamp, 1992

Fairmount gate, 1992

Cell door/cell block 14, 1992

Entry hallway, 1992

STRETCHER, 1992

Seven, 1994

CELL BLOCK 7, 1994

Chair and sunny door, 1993

Rotunda/cell block 7, 1993

**Charles**
*inmate*

When I first came in here, I was scared to death. And from there on in I just took one day at a time, you know. And thank the good Lord I came out the way I came in.

CHAPEL DOOR AND PEW, 1992

Chapel door detail, 1992

Light/cell block 14, 1994

Sun spots, 1994

Cell/cell block 14, 1994

Cell 30, 1994

Guards' tower seen from Death Row, 1996 ➤

**Richard**
*inmate*

My cell was, I guess all the cells was, pretty cold in winter. And hot in summer because of the ventilation. They only had one window up the top. Most of the time I slept on the floor because it was much cooler and that bunk was pretty hard, because it was all steel with that mattress.

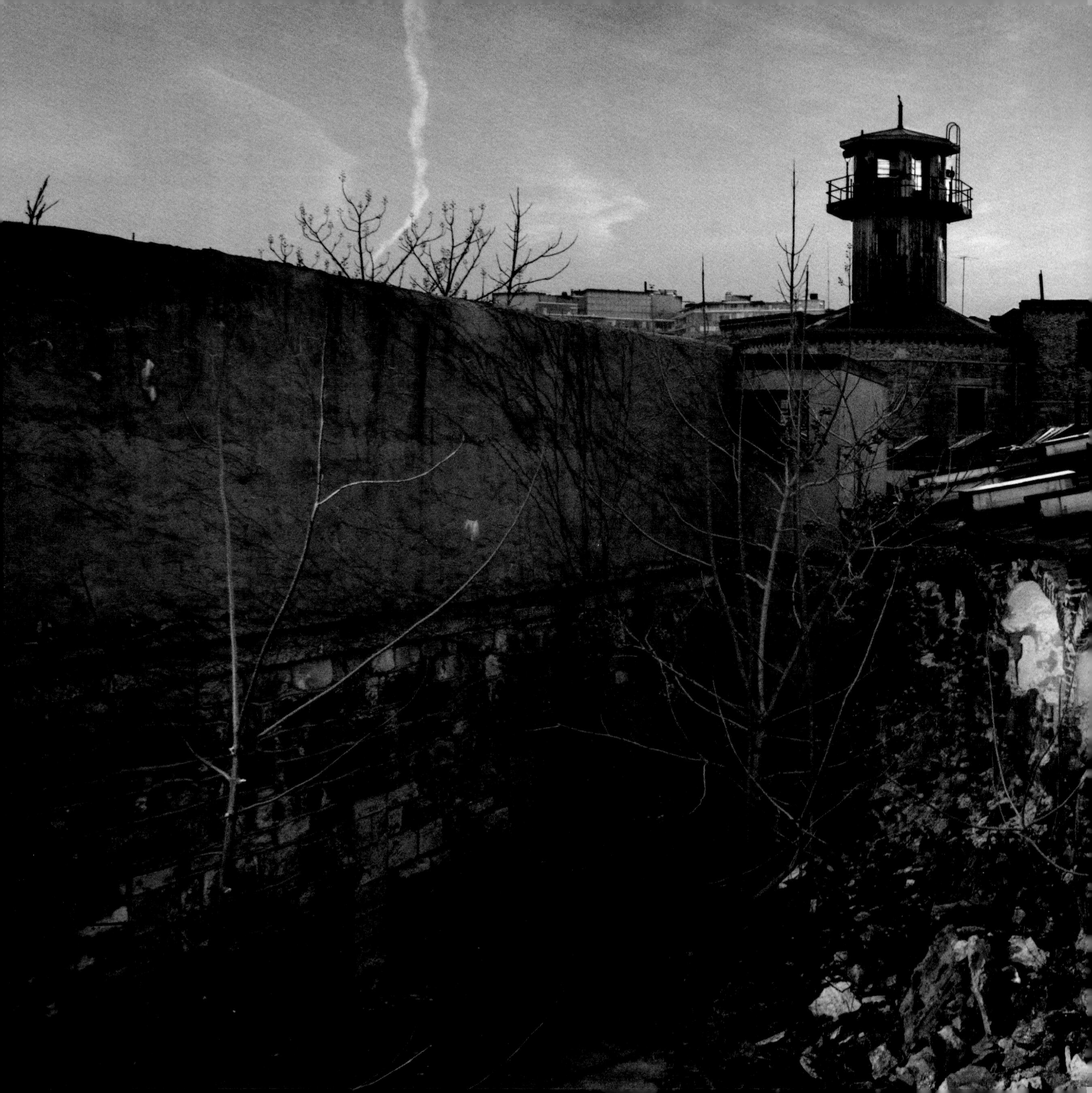

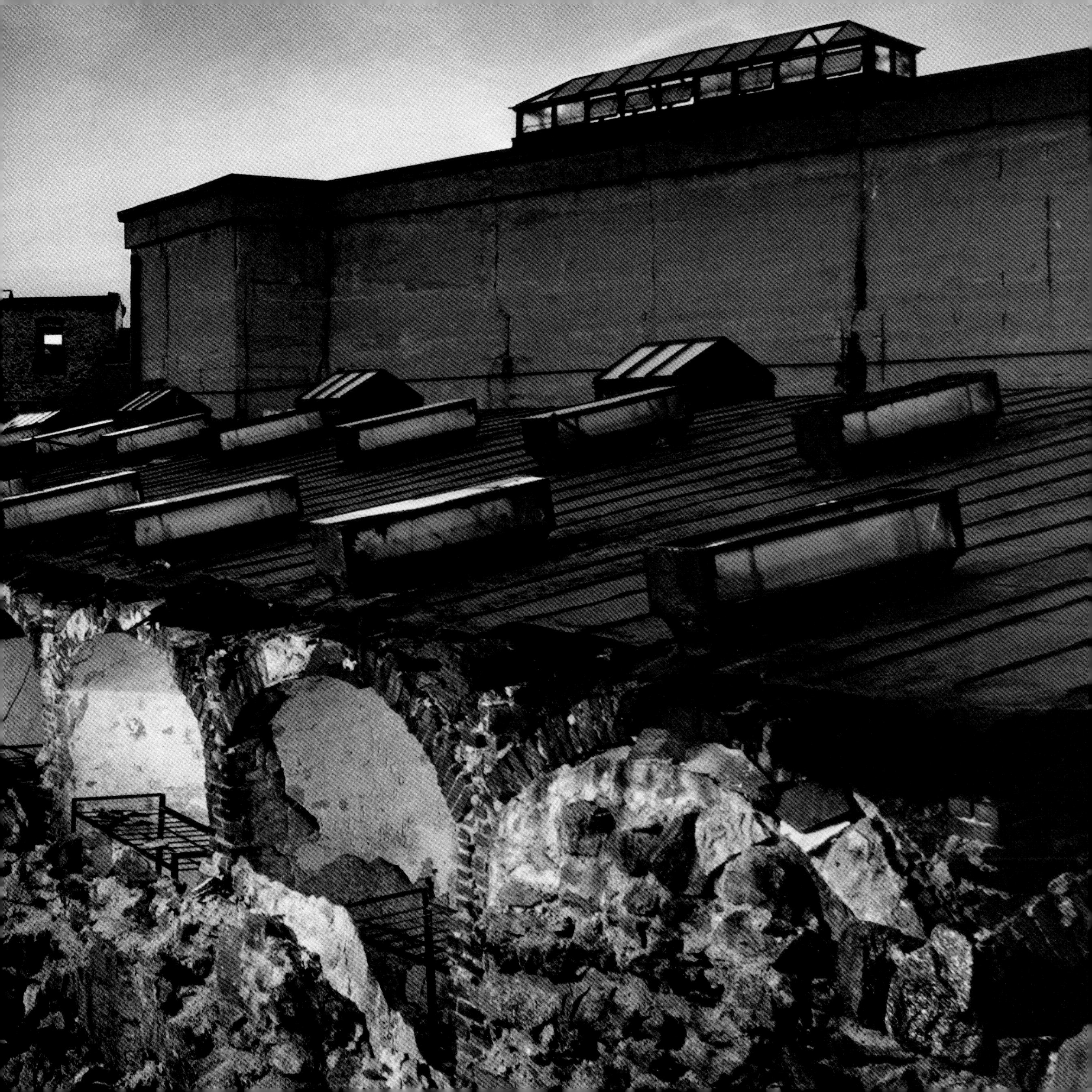

SHOWER, 1992

PRISON SOAPS, 1992

Barber chair, 1994

**Gary**
*son of guard*

When [my father] made lieutenant and captain, I had access to the whole prison. I can remember coming in for no other reason than to play checkers with some of the inmates. I was actually brought in to have a haircut. I remember one inmate who was an inmate barber, and it used to cost me 25 cents for a haircut, and then I'd stay, spend the whole afternoon playing checkers with him. I learned later that he was in for murder.

SHAVING BRUSH, 1994

38

RAZOR BLADES, 1993

**Thomas**
*neighbor*

When the prisoners used to play ball in their Yard, sometimes they would knock the ball over the wall. And then the kids in the neighborhood used to try to throw it back over. It was quite an accomplishment because that's quite a high wall for a young kid to toss the ball over. As we got older and a little bit bigger, our arms became a little more adept at throwing the ball back over the prison wall. We figured it was the proper thing to do.

FOUL BALL LINE, 1993

View down Corinthian, 1993

BASEBALL, 1992

**Raymond**
*neighbor*

I get a chuckle when I hear all of the protests on television today about 'don't put a prison in my back yard!' We grew up with it and I never remember being told 'don't go near the prison' or 'don't talk to the prisoners.' It was just accepted. I mean, we lived here and the prison was here, and if any escapee got over the walls or through the sewers, he wasn't going to hang around here. They would be long gone. So we just never thought much about it.

Wall, 1992

FAIRMOUNT/SNOWY MORNING, 1993

Prisoner's calendar, 1996

**Norman**
*prisoner*

Yes, there were—there were hard times. There were times I laid in bed myself and cried. I could hear people celebrating New Year's outside my wall. New Year's Eve, you know.

Month

S M T W T S
 1 2
3 4 5 6 7 8 9
10 11 12 13 14 15 16
17 18 19 20 21 22 23
24 25 26 27 28

Charm, 1996

SKYLINE, 1993

SEARCHLIGHT, 1992

STRING HANDLED CUP, 1992

PRISON STOOLS, 1996

Fire hose, 1994

Bucket, 1993

**Joe**
*inmate*

I had a little gray mouse I caught one time. A friend of mine worked in the craft shop, so I said 'how about making a little cage up for me.' Well, he made a cage! He made a Taj Mahal. It was a two-level thing with screen on one side, glass on the other. It had a wheel for running around and running around. Well, I put that by my door at night, turned the light out, and I would watch my mouse playing around in there.

Shoes, 1996

Georgina My Love, 1996

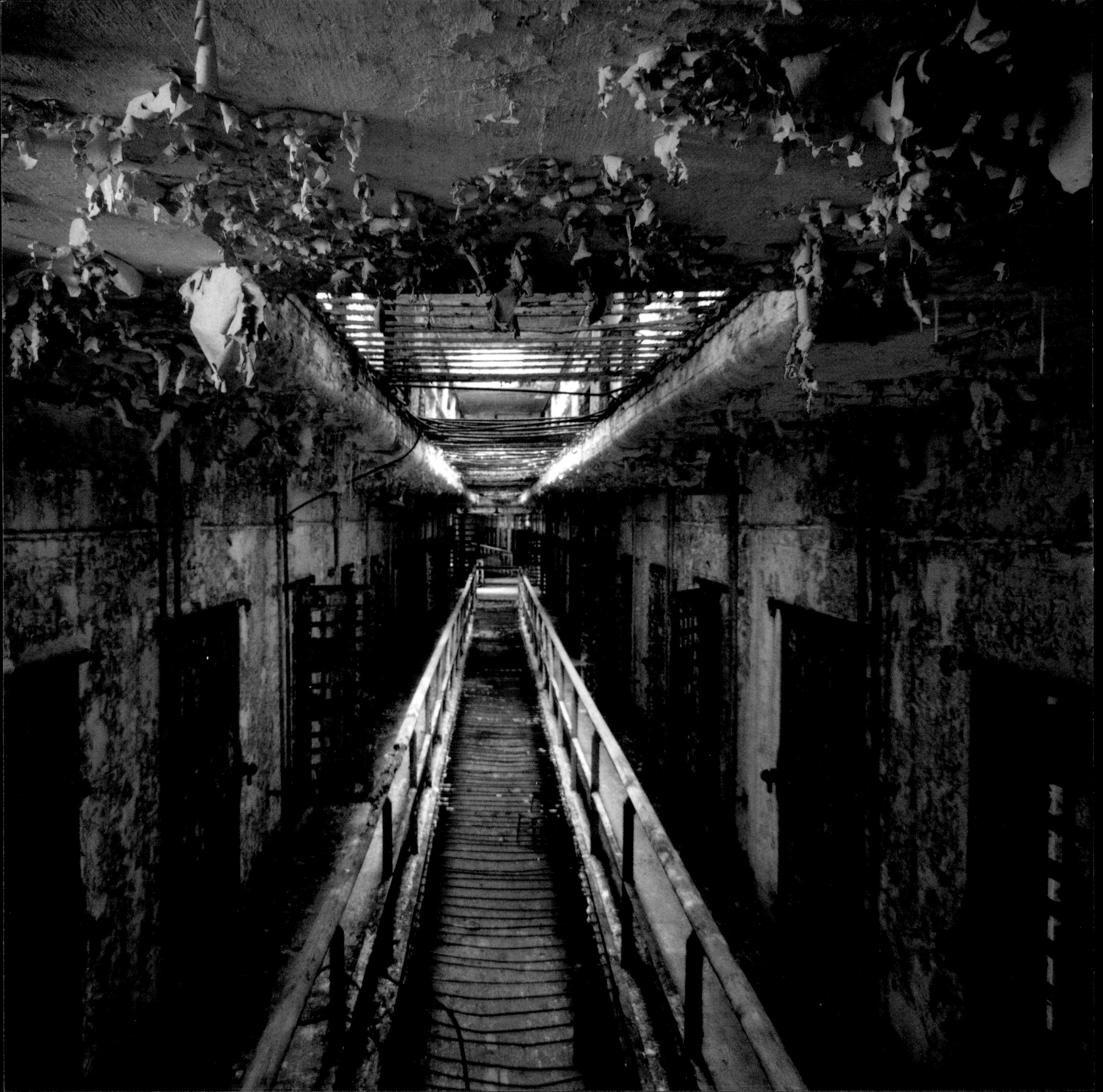

CELL BLOCK 14, 1993

**Jessie**
*inmate*

Gambling was the only thing that kept us alive. And you bet cigarettes. There was no money actually changing hands. You had a foot locker full of cigarettes. You maybe had 200 cartons of cigarettes, and that was your money.

CELL BLOCK 7, 1993

OIL CAN, 1996

Channel C, 1992

CHAPEL AND MOVIE THEATER, 1999

Cell and paulownia roots, 1994

**Dan**
*catman*

What did it look like before? You could eat off these floors. All of these walls were like the inside of your house. Beautiful in here. In that little chapel back there, all of those paintings on the wall that are chipping off and peeling off, they were beautiful. But they just let it go.

Chapel detail, 1993

Thou Art Peter, 1994

CHAPEL, CHAIR, FAN, 1993

CHAPEL SKYLIGHT, 1994

**Elsie**
*daughter of warden who lived inside ESP from 1907 to 1925*

They had religious services and my Dad made them go to church, and, I'm not kidding you, he put his one finger out like this. The men would say that was stronger than a gun. 'You have to go to church.' So they had to go to church. But they respected him for it, because he actually lived what he said. He was very religious. We weren't allowed to read a newspaper on Sunday, nothing… The men wouldn't cook a meal on Sunday, it was cold stuff left from the day before.

STAR, 1994

SYNAGOGUE, 1994

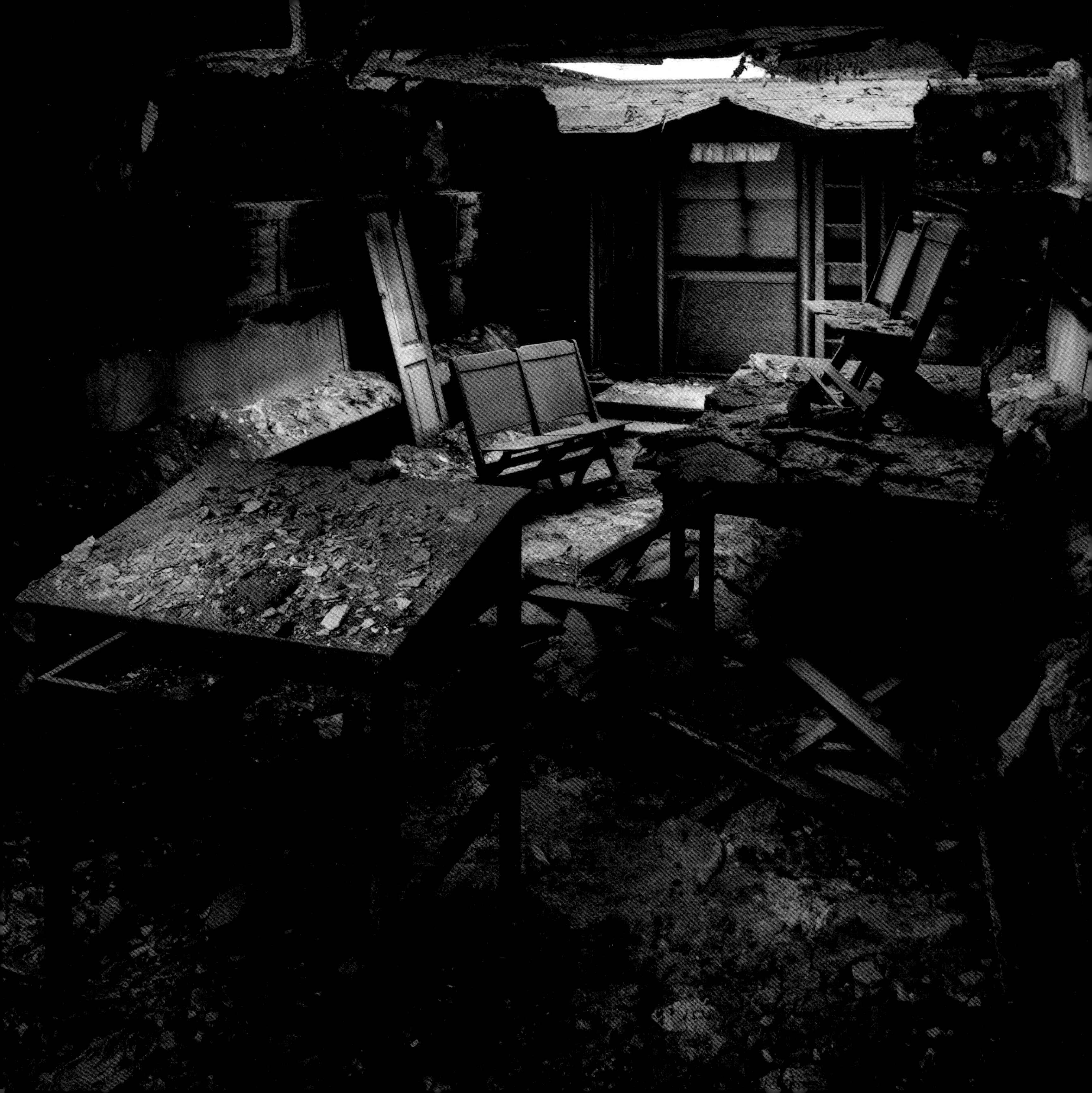

**John** *inmate*

If you hit a guard at that time, the rules was that you got beat all the way to isolation. It wasn't a smack. It wasn't a kick. It wasn't no tie your hands and walk you to isolation. They knocked you down. They kicked you. You had to have either a broken jaw, broken nose, broken arm. So the rules at that time in the early 60s, if you hit an officer or a guard in the prison, you paid the penalty with a broken bone.

PRISON BOOT, 1992

Surgery, 1996

Dr. Goracci's office, 1993

Infirmary bed, 1994

INFIRMARY, 1994

Doorway, warden's quarters, 1996

**Elsie**
*daughter of warden who lived inside ESP from 1907 to 1925*

It was just like home. On the third floor there were two bedrooms and a very, very large sitting room. We would have parties. Oh, I was married there. Right in the big sitting room. I had 250 guests—a sit-down dinner catered by McAllister's. I was married there in 1921 and Andy, my son, was born at the prison. Dr. Ingle, he lived at 20th and Fairmount Avenue, was the doctor. He brought all my babies into the world. All my babies were born home.

**Cochese**
*inmate*

They had good food. I mean good food. Wasn't nothing bad there 'cause I prepared it, and a lot of other guys that worked in the kitchen helped prepare it. We had, we were getting like half a chicken. We didn't get no chicken leg or nothing like that. You got steak, and you got hamburger, which we all made up in the institution, see. They had an inmate who was a baker on the street, and he prepared everything. I forget his name. He was a little short guy, and he was a hell of a baker. He made cinnamon buns, and you name it.

Mess hall, 1996

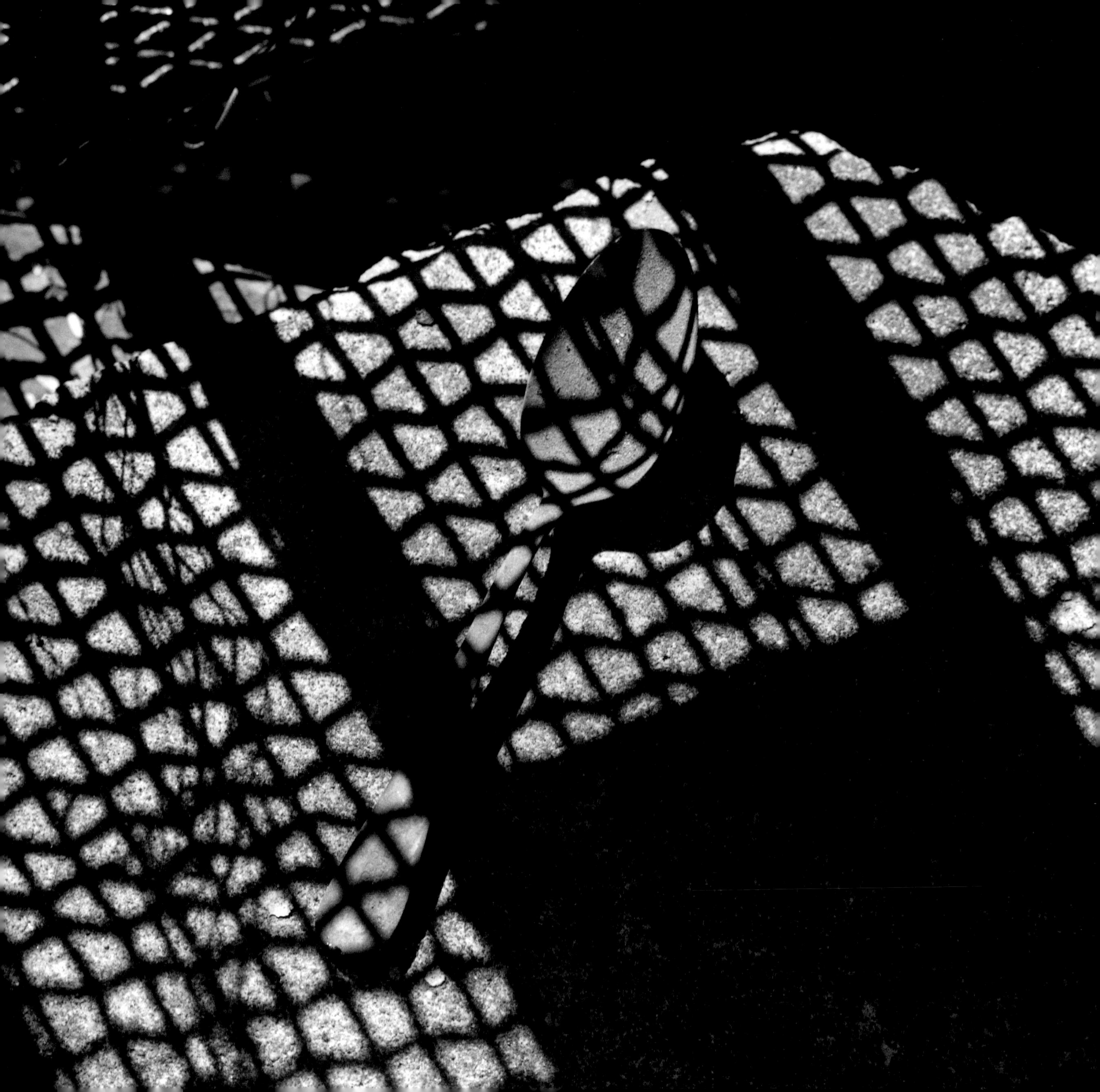

Spoon, 1996

**Jessie**
*inmate*

You didn't have no chef. You had a guy that came in off the street. They taught him how to cook, and he made bean soup. He made bean soup. And you ate it.

Guard's office, 1993

Population/left right, 1993

## 6-G
### LEFT     RIGHT

|  | |
|---|---|
| 2 | H-0313 ALPHONSO LARUE |
| 4 | H-3831 Charles Butler 7:8 |
| 6   LDCC HOUSING | -6976 Emanuel Johnson 7/9 |
| 8 | 5 |
| 10 | 7 |
| 12 | 9   H-1729 GETTIS RILEY |
| 14 | 11 |
| 16 | 13   E-2... WILLIAM THORNTON |
| 18 | 15 |
| 20 | 17 |
| 22 | 19 |
| 24 | 21 |
| 26 | 23   UNDER-REPAIR |
| 28 | 25 |
| 30 | 27 |
| 32 | 29 |
|    | 31 |

## 5-G
### RIGHT

55, 57, 59, 61, 63, 65, 67
1, 3, 5, 7, 9, 11, 13, 15

## 7-G
### LEFT

55, 57, 59, 61, 63, 65, 67
2, 4, 6, 8, 10, 12, 14, 16

(right column) 55, 57, 59, 61, 63, 65, 67, 1, 3, 5, 7, 9, 11, 13, 15

Walkway next to solitary, 1994

The Cool Kidd, 1994                    *detail* ➤

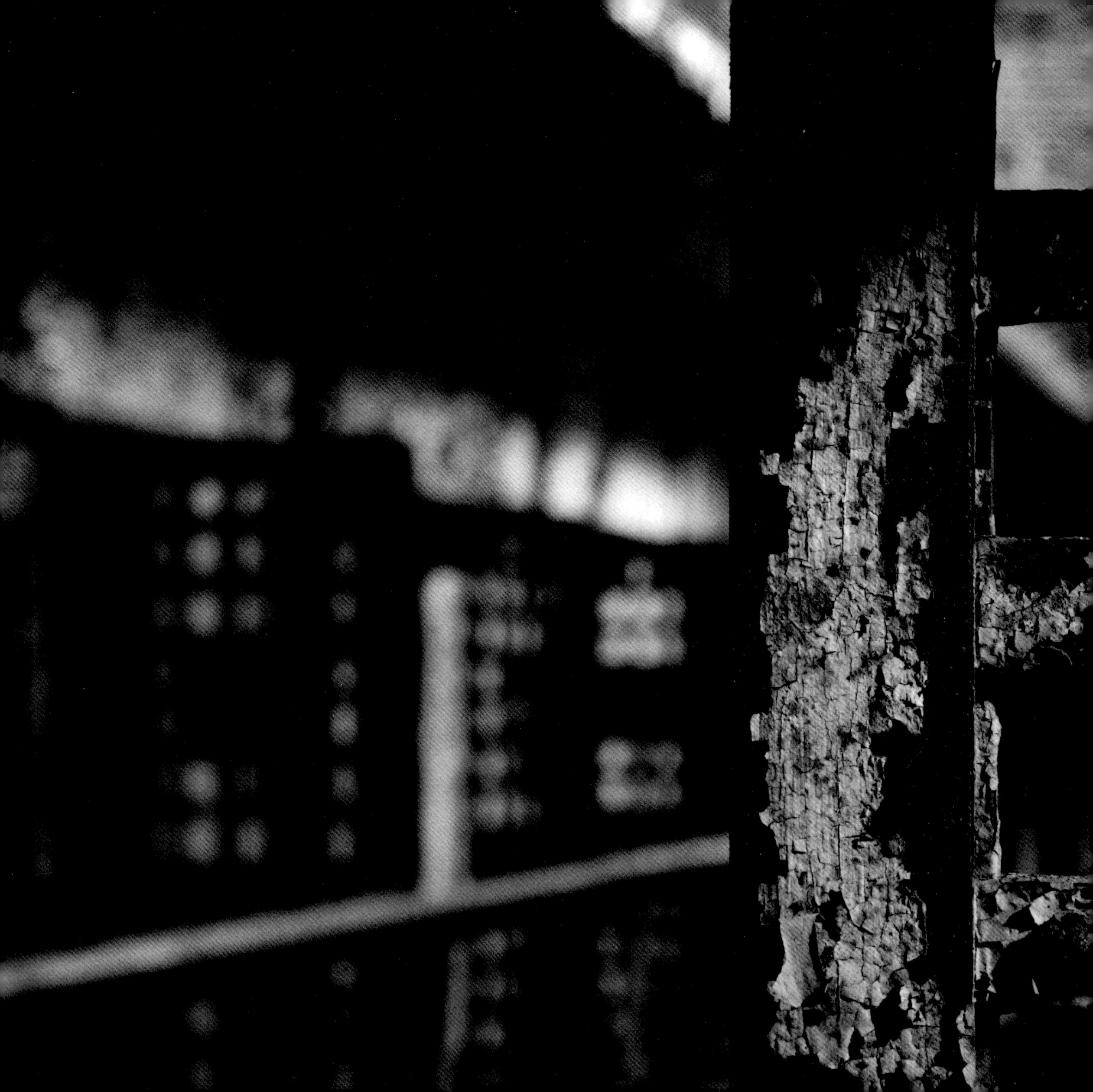

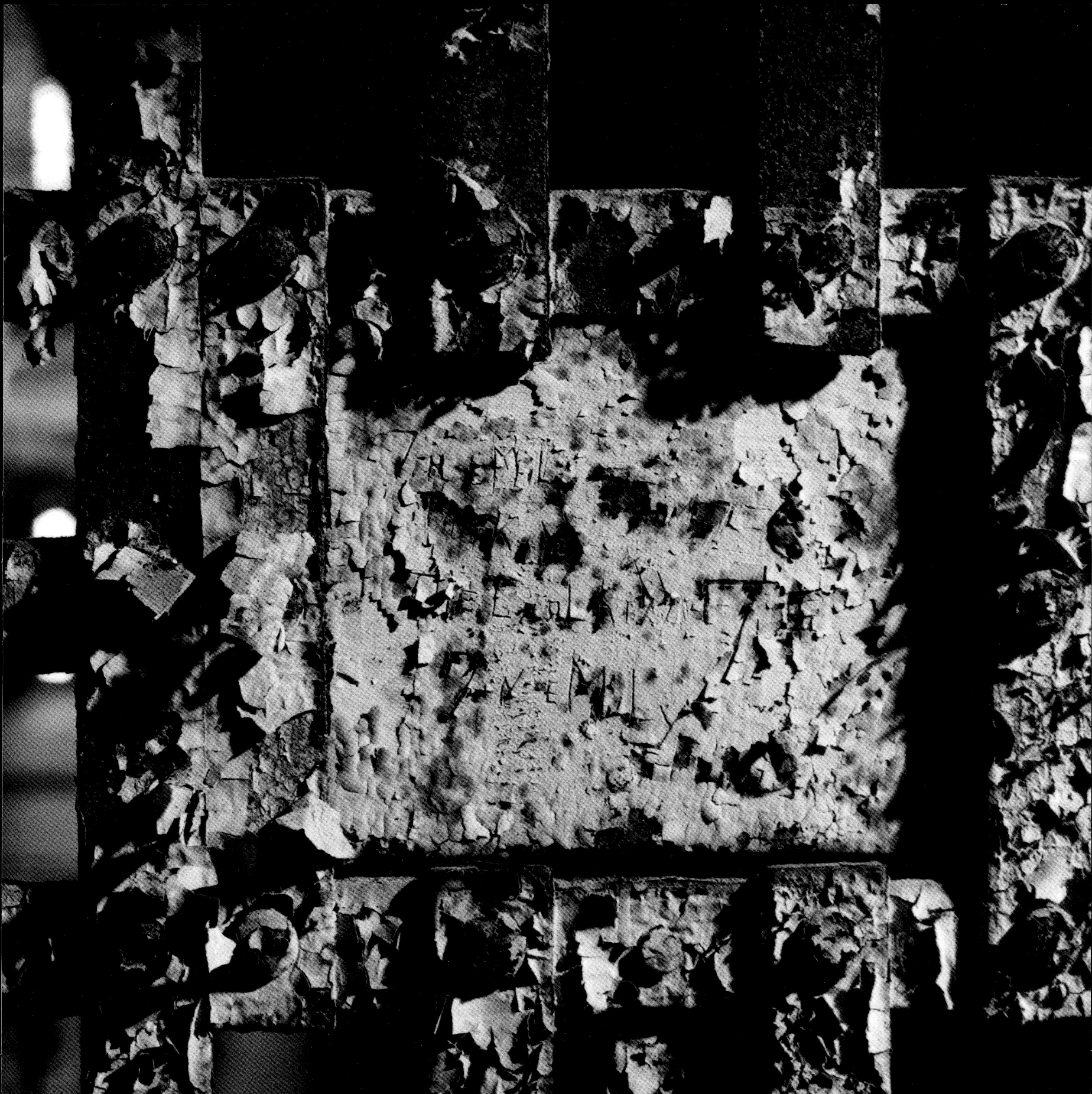

VISITORS' ROOM, 1994

**Jessie**
*inmate*

My mother came up every two weeks. Rain, snow, shine, I don't care what it was. The guys used to bet me. They used to say, 'oh, she ain't coming today, not with all this snow on the ground.' I said, 'I'll be dressed. I'll be waiting for her.' Sure enough, I'd hear my number, and I'd go down there, and there she was. She would be sitting there and leave me my three dollars for cigarettes. And we had our little visit, and she would go home. And that was it.

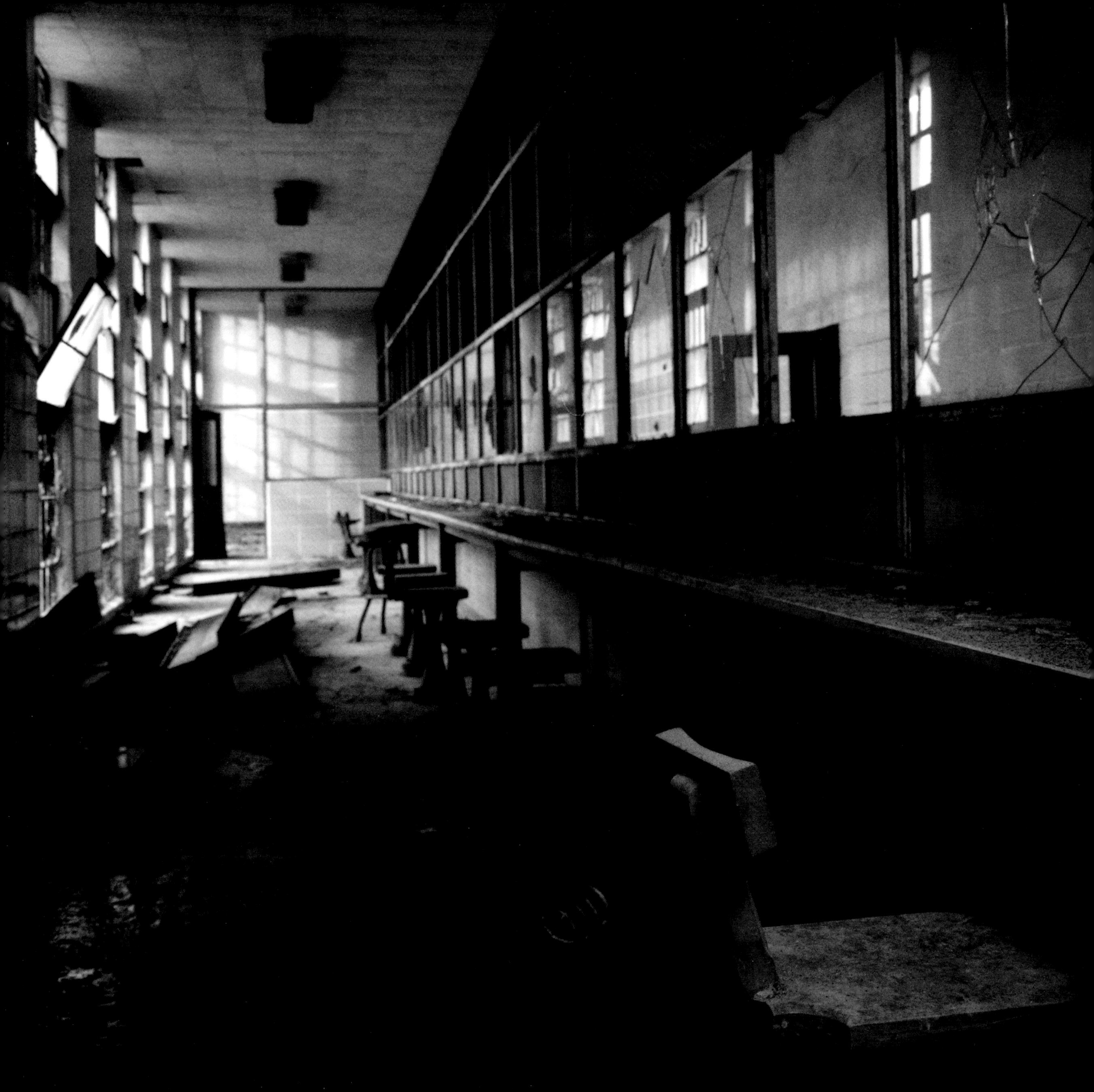

**Lionel**
*neighbor*

I was born and raised in the neighborhood, and my family has lived in the neighborhood dating back to the turn of the century. My family ran a beer distributor opposite the prison. I remember one very hot summer's day we were getting a delivery of kegs of beer when one of them fell off the truck and hit the sidewalk and split open, sending beer about 30 feet into the air. We looked across the street and there was a work gang down on their knees begging for us to aim it over their way.

Fairmount streetscape, 1992

View west, Fairmount, 1992

**Jessie**
*inmate*

They give you a suit when you leave there, which I didn't take. My mother brought my own suit up for me. They have three doors to go through before you can get out to the street. The main door goes into the prison. The car pulls up in there. The door shuts. Then, when that is shut, they open the second one. And then you got the other one that goes out into the street. And once I got out there, I just turned around and looked, and I says 'well, pal, that's the end. You ain't never going to see me again.'

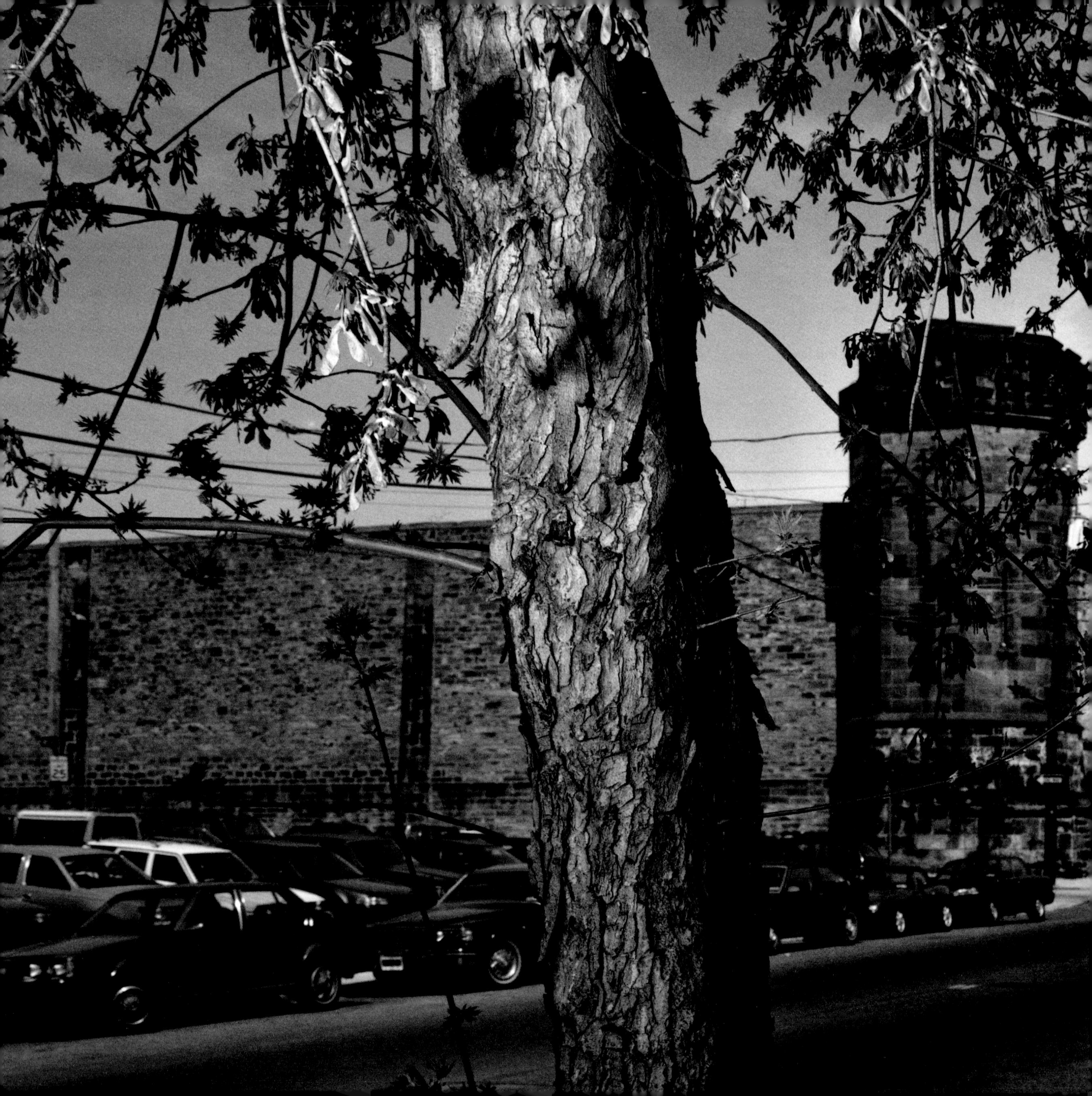
25

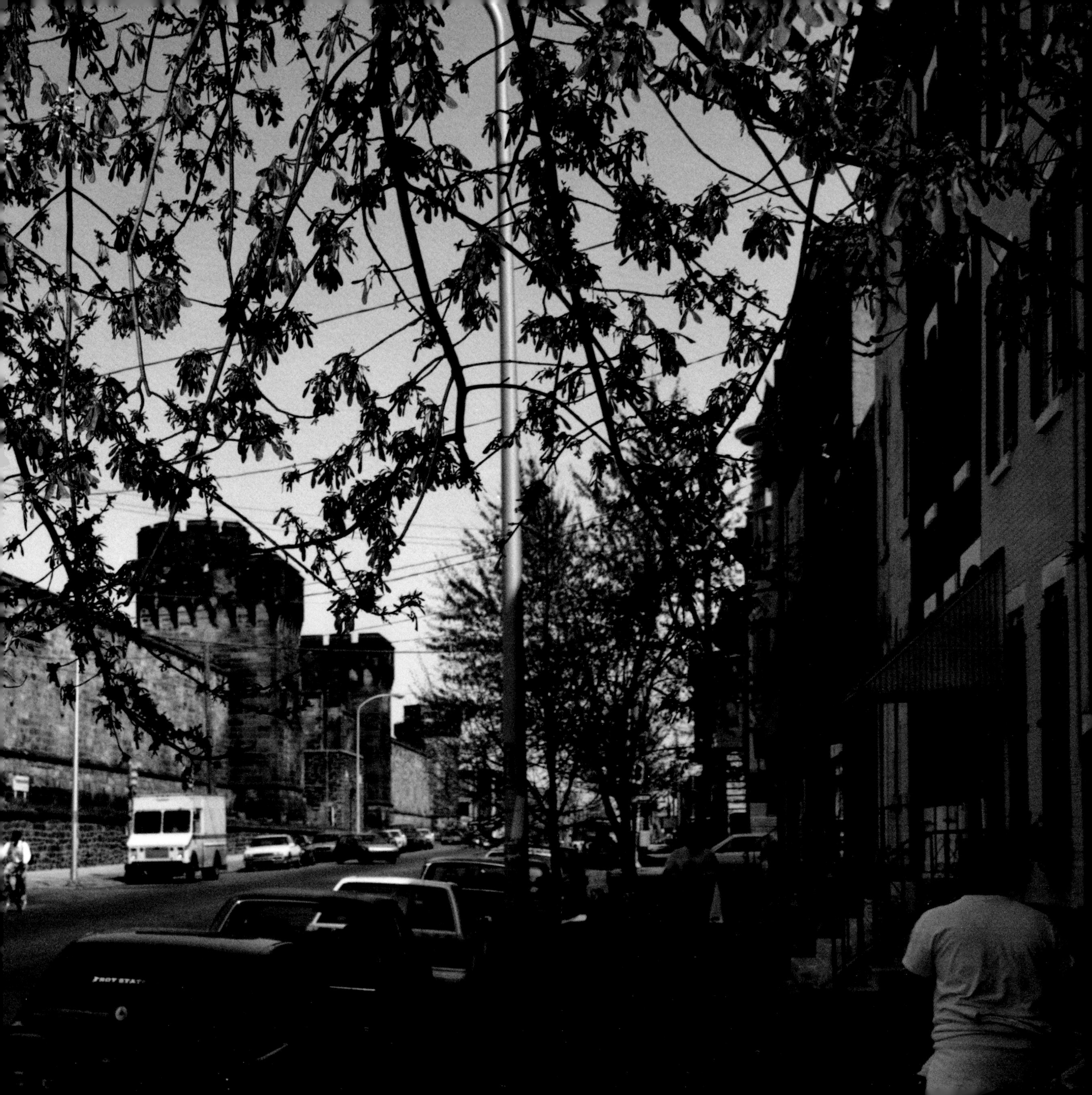

GREENHOUSE, 1994

Skyline, snow, 1993